# Glow

Lynda Charles

# Glow

Copyright © 2018 Lynda Charles

All Rights Reserved

No part of this publication may be reproduced, distributed or transmitted in any form or by any means, including photocopying recording, or other electronic or mechanical methods, without prior written permission of the publisher, except in the case of brief quotations embodied in critical reviews and certain other noncommercial uses permitted by copyright law. For permission requests, write to the publisher at the address below.

ISBN: 978-0-9983676-1-3 (paperback)

LCCN: 2018953093

With a Capital M Publishing Group, LLC

P.O. Box 52656

Durham, NC 27717

www.withacapitalm.com

withacapitalm@gmail.com

Special discounts are available on quantity purchases by corporations, associations, and others. For details, contact the publisher at the address above.

## Dedication

Creator.

Universe.

Spirit.

Mother.

Family.

Friends.

Belief.

Failure.

Experience.

Heartbreak.

Joy.

Midnight hours.

Taverns.

Paper.

Pen.

And you allowed me to be.

                                                  Thanks

## Contents

Opening

Initial

Falling

Firsts

Hurt

In Between

Lessons Learned

Radiance

Opening.

"Don't forget about me." she whispered.
"I won't. How could I?" I responded.
I glanced at her and gave her a tight hug.
"Don't forget to call me." she said.
I packed up my bags of excitement and promises of the future.
I looked out from the window of his car and waved goodbye.
I sighed happily.
I glanced at him and smiled.
"I finally found it!" I whispered to myself.
"I found love."

Day 1: "Hey, sorry I missed your call. I have been busy."

Day 30: "Hey, I will call you back when I get a chance."

Day 60: "I forgot to check in with you. Hope all is well."

Day 120: "I know you haven't heard from me. Just trying to figure out some things out."

Day 160: "I have never been in this place before. It's not like me. Can you pick up?"

Day 180: "Hey, it's me again. He broke up with me. Call me back when you get a chance."

Day 181: "Hi. I'm sorry. I know I abandoned you. But I am broken and in tears right now. I don't even know who I am anymore. I miss you. I need- "

Heart picked up the phone.
"Hi. This is what I have been waiting for."

do not lose yourself in love; take care

So you are happy.
You have not been cracked.
You are whole.
Congratulations.
So whole - you do not realize.
It is only a matter of time...


                        light is always searching

Initial.

Before I met you,
I was a restored blank canvas.
I worked diligently to erase the smudges and smears
of those who left me feeling unworthy.
I was not to be painted again.
Then I met you.
You stained my life the first day we met.


I don't want to ruin you

Rainbows exploding,
colors I never knew existed,
cascading into waves and
crashing against the walls of my heart.

when I first met you

"To whom do I give these flowers to?" she asked.
"To him." I responded.
"Why would you give a man flowers?"
"Because I have always been given skeletons."
"And with this man?"
"He's given me horizon."

          flowers and things

For the stars I was able to see,
The galaxies I danced with,
The meteors I witnessed,
The comets I held.
I praise him with showers and blue skies.
"Why?" she asked.
"Because he showed me light."

reveal

Others have given me skeletons in a closet, while you give me a room full of mirrors.

revelation

I was fighting a losing battle.
My eyes became heavy
and I could not keep them open.
My body stopped tensing up -
began to relax.
I was floating off and hated it.
His arms became home.
He was familiarity.
Comfort.
Something I promised I would never feel with another
man again.
I was no longer in control.

safe

Falling.

I was used to ashes.
Everything I touched fell victim to flame.
So I left fire alone.
Until I met you.
Imagine.

fire is also light

I did not know calm existed.
Until you showed me -
waves do not have to crash against the shore.


float

Tenderness.
I did not know
I could be tender.
Did not know -
I could be this soft.
Until.
You removed the hard edges,
peeled away the rough layers,
and spoke to the thorns.
You touched my petals so delicately.
I was overcome.
And decided to reveal to you.

my rose

You see me.

Not my flaws,

not my imperfections,

not my insecurity,

not my unspoken.

You. see. me.

And dare not to call it less than beautiful.

                                                          eyes for the soul

I used to think I would have to beg for love;
beg for affection,
give myself first,
to be recognized and valued.
Then I met you.
You never asked for any such thing.
You just asked me to be.
And that is all I am doing.

being

I was used to excitement:
blood rising,
pressure racing,
emotions flooding.
That when your peace came -
I was frightened.
Because I was used to lust captivating me,
I did not know love could adorn me.

crown of hearts

For things to happen,
as easily as they have.
For everything to fit together,
as perfect as they have.
For everything to have fallen in place,
as they have.

to whom do I owe the pleasure?

"With him, all I ever touched was bone."
"And with me?"
"With you, I touch horizon."


honest conversations

This moment -
where your heart beats tender.
I trace the outline of your lips.
I place my head across your chest.
Your arms become home.
You breathe soft butterflies.
As you sleep, I am working.
I place my hand on your heart and on mine.
I start to pray.

gratitude

I wrote a list.
Carefully crafted.
Streamed thoughts of pure energy,
authentic desire,
genuine intentions,
and honest trust.
I wrote this list.
Then I burned it.
Instead of receiving ashes -
I received you.

                                        the list: in love's form

First.

You were a series of firsts.
And now...
I don't know how to prepare myself
to turn the page.

end

There is no hell or high water you can move when someone is not meant for you.

when heart speaks to you

Because you were there for the seasons,
I assumed you would be here for a lifetime.


                                    my mistake

The truth is,
I was never intended to be a journey-
just a destination.
Journeys you prepare for;
destinations you travel to only once.


fool's map

I sat and spun woven fabric.
You know -
the soft fabric that cloaks the heart.
Only for you to tell me,
you do not wear cheap clothing.
Ain't that a motherfucker.

seamstress

Hurt.

Suffer.
It is time to pay.


                                        when the bill is due

I marveled at his ability to laugh;
to have such joy.
When I still broke down
at the could have beens.
Until it hit me.
He left long before I realized he was gone.

burn notice

The unborn still cry when I mention you.



plans we will never see

Honor.

Give her honor.

Build her a tabernacle.

Celebrate her.

Worship her.

Offer your heart as tribute.

But do not lay with her.

Do not make her a mother.

your pain

Sit in it.

Dig it.

Scratch it.

Face your tears.

Face the memories.

Face the disappointment.

The hurt.

The hollow.

This pain -

it is uncomfortable.

Let it.

Be uncomfortable in your pain.

                                                comfort check

It comes in waves.
Sometimes loud,
crashing.
Sometimes hurried,
overwhelming.
But lately,
it has been quiet -
subtle.
Almost tolerable.
"What is it?" she asked.
"The pain."


ocean of sorrow

Let it tear at you.

Let it claw at you.

Let it beg for you.

Let it cry for you.

Let it bury you.

But, do not let it consume you.

                                                    monster

Let it spill from your eyes.
Let it spill from your lips.
Let it fall through your hands.
Let it roll off your shoulders.
Let it leave your heart.
Whatever you do though -
do not hold it against its will.


barricading water

For once in your life,
stop trying to escape the brokenness.
Stop trying to evade pain.
Allow yourself to be cracked.
You must experience what it is like
to not be whole.
Sit in the ruins.
Resist the urge to piece back together.
You are in the place of cracks.


scattered and shattered

"It hurts. A part of me feels broken."
Tears rolled down my cheek.
"I know," she said.
"But you will be whole again.
In due time.
For now, pain is your lesson.
You need this pain, Lynda.
You need to learn this lesson."

unwilling student

"What do I do now?"
"Sit!" she screamed.
"Just sit. Sit in it."
"Sit in hurt's lap.
Be quiet.
Listen to the lesson and learn it."


experience speaks

To look at myself in the mirror,
acknowledge the demons,
acknowledge the dirt.
I need a shovel.

ground work

For the breaking,
the suffering,
ignorance,
abandonment,
and betrayal.


apologies to my heart

You will heal.
But you must first taste salt.


                                                    tears

I am hurt.

I am pain.

I am the never agains.

The whys.

The ifs.

I am here.


                              in this place of sorrow

Hurt will always ruin your plans.
Hurt is the reminder
nothing is permanent.


presence

In Between.

I turn on the water in the bathtub.
Unwrap myself of my scars.
I lightly burn oil,
bathe myself with sage.
I wait.
I clothe myself in never agains.
Spray tear-stained perfume.
I look into the mirror and vow to her:
"From this day forward, our choice in men will no longer be regret."

late night affirmations

There are many times I reached out -
only to find my hands wrapped around my heavy
heart.


lonely

You broke my heart with the truth.
Not with lies,
not with what I wanted to hear,
but your truth.


careful what you ask for

"I understand," she said.
"What?" I asked.
"I understand why you love the tavern.
It is quiet in there. "
"The darkness reminds you of what to keep hidden.
But my dear it is time to leave.
Time for light."

refusal

In that moment, I saw her.
She was full of joy -
her heart full of happiness as she held onto her lover's hand.
She beckoned me to come over.
I almost did.
Until I saw the bones she carried in her opposite hand.
When she saw me look down, her smile disappeared.
We both closed our eyes.
I was brought back in.
I opened my eyes.
Tears were streaming down my cheek.
Those were my bones I held in my hand.

facing denial

Don't let darkness be the only time.


                                        value your light

I want to hate you because of your honesty.
But, how can I abhor what set me free?


reluctant

"Sit in that agony.
Sit in that loneliness.
Sit in the pain."
"Why?" I asked.
"Because when you sit,
you shed the weight of the water,
the disappointments
and the hurt."
"Unwrap yourself of it.
Take it off.
This is not becoming of you."

lift the veil

People romanticize the bridge.
The bridge is not a happy place.
It is not filled with love or hope.
It is a place of anxiety;
the bridge is the moment of truth.
The bridge reveals intent.

crossroads

Lessons Learned.

Before bed:
take off the confusion,
wipe away the resentment,
brush away the unanswered questions.
Rub off the conversations that will never happen,
bathe yourself with peace,
let understanding drape your shoulders,
and resolution rest in your lap.
The lesson was meant for you.
Learn it,
then let it go.

prayers before bed

I begged the universe for your love.
Argued with the stars,
clashed with the gods of earth.
It never occurred to me,
you did not want to be involved in the fight.

drafted solider

The gift of honesty.

many do not receive

Time and healing.
Do not deny yourself this.


worth

If it is taken away,
then you did not need it.


hoarder of love and things

I took his love,
placed it on a tabernacle.
Praised and worshipped it every day,
burned sacrifices unconditionally.
Gave tribute.
Not realizing
I was the god to be worshipped.

                                                          false deity

I desperately wanted to lie to him -
to pretend I was okay with remaining friends.
But each conversation made me push the bottle away.
Soon enough I would throw the bottle in the trash and
begin the path of false hope.
With hands shaking and tears trembling,
I told him:
"I cannot do this anymore."
"I do not want to be friends."
"I need space and time to heal."
I hung up the phone.
Bitterly, I swallowed.

pill of truth

The universe has her palm open,
waiting to gift you of her treasure.
Yet you refuse to let go of cheap gold.

cubic zirconia love

"Let go!"
She tried to pry love from my arms.
"No!" I shouted.
"This is mine! It's mine. I deserve this. It's my time!"
I violently pushed her into the pavement
and tucked love into my back pocket.
I watched as she fell to the ground.
The black box she was carrying split open.
She screamed in horror as a constellation
of rare stars and blue moons spilled from the box.
They quickly turned into dust.
I stood there mesmerized.
Never had I witnessed something so beautiful.
"Who was that for?" I asked her.
Tears decorated her cheeks.
The universe whispered,
"I heard your cries and prayers.
Went searching through the skies and the galaxies."


universe hears: these were for you

"Oh dear."

"It is coming."

"The time when heart, mind, body and soul unite.

To make the decision.

To leave.

For good."

breaking point

"Eventually you will have to let go."
"What if I do not want to?" I asked.
She lit up a cigarette.
"Don't worry darling.
Life has a forceful habit of giving us bones
when we really want flowers."


cigarette conversations

Women desire to give birth.
To love,
to tenderness,
to vulnerability.
They wind up miscarrying
because of the men they choose to conceive with.


                                                    motherhood

Men hunger too.
For love,
for peace,
for stability.
Yet, they starve to death
because of the women they choose to feast with.


men's famine

I did not know he danced with angels during the day
and slept with demons at night.
He hid his wars so well.


                                        internal battle

I knew there was a battle going on...
His actions told a different story than his mouth.


the wars your mother warns you about

I have given my all to men
who would not give me half.


                              love you to pieces

I tend to have a habit of sewing garments for men
who would never appreciate the material.

seamstress part two

I have healed countless hearts
with only mine still broken.

gypsy

The mouth has nothing to hide.
It is the heart we need to look after.
For the mouth will always tell on the heart.
But we cannot see a person's heart.


church, friends, and conversation

"Above all else, I want him to be happy."
"Even if it is without me."
"And that is the greatest pain of all."
"What?" she asked
"Acknowledging happiness no longer rests with me,
but in the arms of another."


hold

"When it is time to give up, you will know."
"How?" I asked.
"It is quite simple dear."
She took off her glasses.
"When your eyes can no longer support the stream of the oceans at night.
When your hands can no longer hold the walls in between.
When your mind fatigues from the many miles you walk during the day."
"What about your heart?" I asked her.
She briefly smiled.
"Oh sweetheart, our heart always knows when it is time to move on.
Our hearts often know the answer.
We just choose to ignore it."

ignorance is bliss

She poured herself a drink.
"Trust me dear, almost doesn't count.
You never want to be half loved."
"I have been half loved. All it ever did was leave me in a perpetual state of want, because I never got what I needed."
She sipped her drink and continued,
"Always stuck in the in-betweens.
Just waiting. Waiting to be complete.
Waiting for purpose - to be full instead of empty."
She stopped for a moment and sighed.
"To be fulfilled. Oh, to be fulfilled!
Darling you deserve to be filled.
You deserve overflow. "

milk and honey

Radiance.

She took her hand a placed it in mine.
"Do not worry," she said.
"You will get through this."
"How?" I asked.
She unbuttoned her blouse.
I saw scars from where all the incisions were made.
She smiled.
"Because I did."

my heart

You.
Are a great work.
A wonder among the stars.
A god of the many universes we travel through our lifetime.
Do not shrink.

majestic power

Just as your breath comes to you each morning,
as your eyes open to greet a new day,
so flows the course of a love that is meant for you.
If that has not happened yet,
do not be alarmed.
It is simply not your time.

patience

It is okay to hurt.

But while in the process of grieving,

do not deny yourself the time to heal.

You are worthy of restoration.

note to self

How do women do it?
Carry oceans in our eyes and sunrises in our smiles?
How do we carry beauty in brokenness?


the strength in our backs

Oh beautiful flower.
The world marvels at your wonder
and would bow at your feet.
Yet you concern yourself with your broken petals.

irrelevant

What flowers have you given yourself?
How is your heart today?

self care check

Women.
Love and air.
Have in common:
To feel light.


read again

You have a right.

To burn.

To radiate.

Light is your own.

So glow.

Glow

I was expecting a shattering of sorts:
A thunderstorm.
Or perhaps a roar from the universe.
What I received instead,
was soft and quiet.
It was warm.
Radiance I never felt before.
A glow.

Glow II

And so it is.

www.ingramcontent.com/pod-product-compliance
Lightning Source LLC
Chambersburg PA
CBHW061957070426
42450CB00011BA/3123